Samuel French Acting Edition

Middle Class, Too

by Brad Slaight

SAMUELFRENCH.COM   SAMUELFRENCH.CO.UK

Copyright © 2019 by Brad Slaight
All Rights Reserved

MIDDLE CLASS, TOO is fully protected under the copyright laws of the United States of America, the British Commonwealth, including Canada, and all other countries of the Copyright Union. All rights, including professional and amateur stage productions, recitation, lecturing, public reading, motion picture, radio broadcasting, television and the rights of translation into foreign languages are strictly reserved.

ISBN 978-0-573-70783-4

www.SamuelFrench.com
www.SamuelFrench.co.uk

FOR PRODUCTION ENQUIRIES

UNITED STATES AND CANADA
Info@SamuelFrench.com
1-866-598-8449

UNITED KINGDOM AND EUROPE
Plays@SamuelFrench.co.uk
020-7255-4302

Each title is subject to availability from Samuel French, depending upon country of performance. Please be aware that *MIDDLE CLASS, TOO* may not be licensed by Samuel French in your territory. Professional and amateur producers should contact the nearest Samuel French office or licensing partner to verify availability.

CAUTION: Professional and amateur producers are hereby warned that *MIDDLE CLASS, TOO* is subject to a licensing fee. Publication of this play(s) does not imply availability for performance. Both amateurs and professionals considering a production are strongly advised to apply to Samuel French before starting rehearsals, advertising, or booking a theatre. A licensing fee must be paid whether the title(s) is presented for charity or gain and whether or not admission is charged. Professional/Stock licensing fees are quoted upon application to Samuel French.

No one shall make any changes in this title(s) for the purpose of production. No part of this book may be reproduced, stored in a retrieval system, or transmitted in any form, by any means, now known or yet to be invented, including mechanical, electronic, photocopying, recording, videotaping, or otherwise, without the prior written permission of the publisher. No one shall upload this title(s), or part of this title(s), to any social media websites.

For all enquiries regarding motion picture, television, and other media rights, please contact Samuel French.

MUSIC USE NOTE

Licensees are solely responsible for obtaining formal written permission from copyright owners to use copyrighted music in the performance of this play and are strongly cautioned to do so. If no such permission is obtained by the licensee, then the licensee must use only original music that the licensee owns and controls. Licensees are solely responsible and liable for all music clearances and shall indemnify the copyright owners of the play(s) and their licensing agent, Samuel French, against any costs, expenses, losses and liabilities arising from the use of music by licensees. Please contact the appropriate music licensing authority in your territory for the rights to any incidental music.

IMPORTANT BILLING AND CREDIT REQUIREMENTS

If you have obtained performance rights to this title, please refer to your licensing agreement for important billing and credit requirements.

MIDDLE CLASS, TOO was developed in workshop by the Young Conservatory of American Conservatory Theater in San Francisco, California in 2017.

SUGGESTED CAST

6m, 12f

OPTIONAL CAST

Because of the number of scenes and characters, you can use more performers than the suggested cast or even less. The scenes are such that cast members can each play multiple roles depending on your casting needs.

TIME

The present

AUTHOR'S NOTES

The Set
The set can be as simple or complex as you wish to make it. In the script I have suggested simple cubes that can be stacked and moved around to create simulated set pieces, seating, and even lockers. You may also choose to go with a "two color" set that reflects your school colors.

Music
You could use transitional music between some of the scenes, as well as sound effects and mood music during some of the scenes.*

Costumes
Basic school clothes and suggestive props.

Additional Notes
The scenes are arranged in a suggested order, however you may change the order if you find it necessary.

Any reference to "middle school" in the play may be changed to "junior high" if that is what your school is called.

---

*A license to produce *Middle Class, Too* does not include a performance license for any third-party or copyrighted music. Licensees should create an original composition or use music in the public domain. For further information, please see Music Use Note on page 3.

Open

*(A lone **STUDENT** takes the stage in darkness. The first light we see is from the screen of their cell phone. He or she begins to text and will speak what they are texting.)*

STUDENT #1. I can't believe I'm finally here. Hashtag: First Day Of Middle School.

*(**STUDENT #2** enters, also with a cell phone, and begins texting. Other **STUDENTS** will continue to enter throughout the scene.)*

STUDENT #2. This place smells like a hospital! Hashtag: Already Sick.

STUDENT #3. Wish my mom hadn't dropped me off. Hashtag: Not A Kid Anymore.

STUDENT #4. I think I saw Mr. Jensen pull into the parking lot. Hashtag: My Brother Said He Is Really Mean.

STUDENT #5. I hear if you make eye contact with him you get detention. Hashtag: Be Afraid.

STUDENT #6. Do we get recess here? Hashtag: Asking For A Friend.

STUDENT #7. What have I gotten myself into! Hashtag: What Have I Gotten Myself Into.

STUDENT #8. ROTFLMAO. Quit bein' a wimpoid! Hashtag: Grow A Pair.

STUDENT #9. What time is lunch? Hashtag: Priorities.

STUDENT #10. Who wants to be my first date ever? Hashtag: Hello Ladies.

STUDENT #11. As if. U R not dating until U graduate high school. Ha! Hashtag: U Neva Been Kissed.

STUDENT #12. Homework, homework, homework! Hashtag: My Sister Says It Is Endless.

STUDENT #13. There go R weekends! Hashtag: Sweatshop.

STUDENT #14. So does this mean I'm a grown-up now? Hashtag: Not Sure I Want To Be.

STUDENT #15. No we R still kids. Hashtag: Nothing Changes.

STUDENT #16. Can't we just skip this and go right to high school? Hashtag: I Want To Get To The Good Stuff.

STUDENT #17. Speaking of skipping. Wanna skip the first day of middle school? Hashtag: Serious.

STUDENT #16. No way. Maybe tomorrow though. Hashtag: Check It Out First.

STUDENT #18. The books seem a lot thicker than last year's. Hashtag: I'm Gonna Need A Bigger Backpack!

> *(The* **STUDENTS** *start ad-libbing texts and talking over each other. This will build in intensity until they are interrupted by a loud class bell. There is a brief, panicked pause and then:)*

ALL. Hashtag: I'm Not Ready For This.

> *(As they break apart and head for the exits, two of the students,* **MIA** *and* **NATALIE**, *look confused as they stare at their phones. They run into each other because they are not looking where they are walking.)*

Scene One

NATALIE. Oh I'm so sorry.

MIA. No that was my fault. I totally was looking at my map thingy...

NATALIE. Map?

MIA. Yes, of the school. I'm new here...this is a GPS app my parents got me so I could find my way around this school. It's called...

NATALIE. "Get To Class"!

MIA. You've heard of it?

NATALIE. I have it on my phone. This is my first day here, too.

MIA. Wow. Glad I'm not the only one. What grade are you in?

NATALIE. Seventh.

MIA. Me, too. I transferred here from Ohio. My pops got a new job.

NATALIE. I was home-schooled but finally talked my parents into letting me go to a real school.

MIA. I was trying to figure out where Mr. Belmondo's classroom is.

NATALIE. This is getting freaky. So was I?

MIA. Brilliant, we're in the same class!

NATALIE. If we can find it. I think the app is off because it keeps telling me to go to the teacher's lounge.

MIA. Yeah, I actually went there twice. Too chicken to ask a teacher or anyone else where his classroom is.

NATALIE. Terrible app!

MIA. I think I heard someone say his classroom is close to the gym. So maybe we should head over that way.

NATALIE. Good idea. Between the two of us I bet we can find it. And if I'm going to be late I'd rather be late with someone else.

MIA. Me too. Oh, my name is Mia.

NATALIE. Natalie.

MIA. I can't tell you how glad I am to run into you…literally… on my first day.

NATALIE. *(Pointing.)* I think the gym is that way.

MIA. I think so, too.

> *(They exit.)*

Scene Two

*(**REBECCA** enters.)*

REBECCA. Does anybody know where I can buy a time machine? Amazon? eBay? Craigslist? Because this middle school thing isn't working out. I'm only in sixth grade so it's gonna be forever before I get to the good part of my life. You know; the fun stuff. Driving, staying out later, the prom, class rings, sweet sixteen parties, and all the other stuff that happens in high school and not here! I have a calendar at home and every day I cross off one more day but I might as well just carve it into the wall like some inmate because I am in a prison known as middle school. My dad was complaining about his job the other day and how time just drags for him when he's there. Oh really? Amateur! I hold the world record for time dragging. At least when he's done he's free to do anything he wants. I have to ride a bus home, do hours of homework, and can't go anywhere on a school night unless I throw myself at the mercy of the Mom and Dad court. So I ask one more time…does anybody know where I can buy a time machine? Because I will transport myself right past the next couple of years faster than my mom drives to the mall for a going-out-of-business sale. Oh and if you do find such a machine, please keep in mind that I can't pay much for it because I only get $5.00 allowance a week. $5.00! Seriously?

(She looks at watch.)

Oh great, I'm not even halfway through this day yet and it's only Monday!

(She storms off.)

Scene Three

*(**ANTHONY** enters and looks around. Stops. Holds his phone up in front of his face.)*

ANTHONY. *(To cell phone camera.)* Tuesday, September twenty-fifth, 12:30 p.m. The cafeteria food today was KINDA like the weather: Cloudy and cold with a chance of mystery meat!

(He lowers the phone and talks to the audience.) Oh, hi, that was one of my video selfies. Mrs. Ritter gave us what she calls a long-term assignment. Goes like this...over the course of the school year, write down something every day that happens in school. Then at the end of the year we'll have our own personal diary of memories that years later we can look back on. I decided to do things a little different. Video selfies. Every day I will record my thoughts and then at the end of the year edit them together so that my words aren't just on a page, but I can see my expression and hear my attitude. My memories will be in living HD. Hopefully future Anthony will appreciate what I'm doing now.

*(Two trendy looking **GIRLS** walk past him.)*

ANTHONY. Lookin' good ladies.

GIRL #1. Nobody asked you, derp.

*(They exit. **ANTHONY** lifts his phone back up to record another video selfie.)*

ANTHONY. Tuesday, September twenty-fifth, 12:33 p.m. Seventh-grade girls are way too full of themselves. Their loss!

*(Satisfied with his entry, **ANTHONY** puts his cell phone in his pocket and exits.)*

Scene Four

(SOPHIA spots ISABELLA running down the hall. ISABELLA is holding a bag.)

SOPHIA. Isabella!
ISABELLA. Sophia!
SOPHIA. Running?
ISABELLA. Late!
SOPHIA. Class?
ISABELLA. Date!
SOPHIA. Now?
ISABELLA. Lunch.
SOPHIA. Ethan?
ISABELLA. Yes!
SOPHIA. Finally.
ISABELLA. Right?
SOPHIA. Cafeteria?
ISABELLA. Courtyard.
SOPHIA. Food?
ISABELLA. *(Holds up bag.)* McDonald's?
SOPHIA. Hot?
ISABELLA. Fresh.
SOPHIA. How?
ISABELLA. Mom!
SOPHIA. Nice.
ISABELLA. Bye.

(ISABELLA exits.)

SOPHIA. Enjoy.

(SOPHIA notices JAYDEN, who walks by. Stops. He sniffs the air.)

JAYDEN. Cheeseburger!
SOPHIA. Yes.
JAYDEN. *(Sniffs again.)* Fries?

SOPHIA. Salty!
JAYDEN. Where?
SOPHIA. Cafeteria!
JAYDEN. Now?
SOPHIA. Hurry!

    *(**JAYDEN** excitedly sprints off. **SOPHIA** smirks.)*

Idiot.

    *(**SOPHIA** exits.)*

Scene Five

(**BRYCE** *enters.*)

BRYCE. My Uncle Larry came over for dinner last night and he said he wishes he was my age again because I have no worries. I almost choked on my meatloaf at that. Why is it that adults have forgotten what it's like to be this age and think they had no worries back then? Because I sure do…

I worry that I'm going to get zits like my older brother.

I worry that the endless pile of homework will never get done.

I worry that Lisa will never notice that I'm the guy for her.

I worry that my gym teacher will find out that I skip taking showers.

I worry that the metal detectors and added security guards won't be able to stop some nutjob from getting in here and shooting up the place.

I worry that I won't get the new sneakers that I want.

I worry that Mr. Kincaid will continue his mission of making my life miserable for the entire school year.

I worry that I will never go through puberty.

I worry that my bike will get stolen.

I worry that this school year will never end and I'll be caught in an endless loop of middle school.

I worry that no one will ever take what I have to say seriously.

And most of all, I worry that I will end up like my Uncle Larry and forget this moment and what this time in my life was really like.

(**BRYCE** *exits.*)

Scene Six

*(**KYLE** enters. He is wearing a jacket and tie but also jeans and sneakers. **HANNAH** walks past him and stops.)*

HANNAH. Whoa! Where you goin'?

KYLE. Math class.

HANNAH. Are you getting an award or something?

KYLE. What?

HANNAH. The tie. Jacket.

KYLE. So what's wrong with wearing a jacket and tie to school.

HANNAH. Because the only ones who do that are teachers... and most of them don't even do that anymore.

KYLE. I figure now that I'm in middle school, I'm like an adult.

HANNAH. Uh, no, like you're not.

KYLE. Certainly on the edge of it anyway.

HANNAH. Or the edge of insanity.

KYLE. It's about growing up, Hannah. When you're looking mature, you're feeling mature.

HANNAH. Sounds like a commercial.

KYLE. This is a man's style and I'm proud to wear it. Last night I was thinking about how people take you more serious when you dress more serious. I have big plans for my adult Kyle future which is coming on fast. I'm going to be a successful businessman like my dad. Actually, I borrowed one of his ties. When I put it on I swear it aged me twenty years just looking at myself in the mirror. I liked how I looked and how I felt. It's like an instant shot of maturity. Some of these kids around here amuse me, but I am destined for greater and grown-up things.

*(**JACOB** enters. He holds several water balloons.)*

JACOB. Hey Kyle, big water balloon fight going on right now!

KYLE. Where?

JACOB. Locker room.

> (**KYLE** *thinks for a minute. Takes a balloon from* **JACOB.** *They start to head off.* **KYLE** *stops. Removes his tie and hands it to* **HANNAH.**)

KYLE. Keep this for me...I don't want it to get wet.

> (**KYLE** *joins* **JACOB.**)

Let's do this!

> (*They whoop it up as they exit.* **HANNAH** *looks after them and shakes her head. She wads up the tie and puts it in her bag.*)

Scene Seven

(AVA enters and spots ELLA, who sits on one of several cubes. ELLA immediately becomes uncomfortable, awaits confrontation.)

ELLA. What do you want?

AVA. I just want to talk.

ELLA. Yeah, right?

AVA. I'm serious.

ELLA. I'll give you one minute. I don't have time for your b.s. today.

(AVA shows ELLA a picture on her cell phone.)

Who's that?

AVA. It's a girl that goes to my cousin's school. I don't know her but he does…or he did.

ELLA. What do you mean "did"?

AVA. She committed suicide last night.

ELLA. That's terrible.

AVA. It gets worse. She took her life because she was bullied by a lot of the kids at his school.

ELLA. Oh…

AVA. Look, Ella, I know I'm not a good person. I mean… I kinda treat people bad sometimes… I kinda treat you bad.

ELLA. Kinda?

AVA. Okay, real bad. I make fun of your clothes…and your family…and the people you hang with…and…

ELLA. Yeah, I know. You don't need to give me the list.

AVA. I just wanted to say…I'm…well… I apologize…for all of the times that I have. And I won't do it anymore.

ELLA. You're just spooked because you think if I off myself you'll be blamed for it.

AVA. Maybe that's part of it. But it's bigger than that. After talking to my cousin last night it really got me thinking…

ELLA. Don't worry. I don't let what you or some of the other kids say to me change who I am.

AVA. I admire that. Something changed for me last night. I mean there are so many bad things in the world...and good things, too...that well, it just isn't right for me to pick on other people.

ELLA. Yeah, I know. You're not that great yourself...

(Beat.)

(Off **AVA***'s reaction.)* I'm kidding. Look I appreciate your apology. But I'd be a fool if I think you won't slip back into the real Ava when this blows over for you. And that's okay. I can take it.

AVA. You won't have to. At least not from me. I swear. And I want you to let me know if I ever do anything that makes you feel bad.

> *(***ELLA*** looks at her for a moment, senses her sincerity. She picks up* **AVA***'s cell phone and looks at the picture again.)*

ELLA. So sad. It's weird how we always have to smile in our school pictures. They just want us to hide how we really feel about life I guess.

AVA. Yeah. I never thought of it that way. You're pretty smart...

> *(A few* **STUDENTS** *walk by and notice the two of them sitting together. They are puzzled.)*

STUDENT #1. Hey Ava, come on we're going to the library...

AVA. I'll meet you there.

(To **ELLA.***)* You want to join us?

ELLA. Uh, no thanks.

(Beat.)

Look, I know we're not going to be friends or anything, but thanks for taking time to...talk.

AVA. Thanks for listening.

(Brief, awkward pause.)

AVA. So, I'll see you around I guess.

ELLA. Sure.

> (**AVA** *exits to join her friends.* **ELLA** *thinks about what happened for a moment, gives a bit of a smile, and then heads off in the opposite direction.)*

Scene Eight

(CHLOE paces back and forth as she writes on a notepad. MAKAYLA, SARAH, and LAUREN enter with a sense of urgency.)

MAKAYLA. What's wrong?

SARAH. Yeah, what's the emergency, Chloe?

CHLOE. I didn't make the cheerleading squad.

LAUREN. Sad, but not really an emergency.

CHLOE. You didn't make it either.

LAUREN. Thanks for reminding me.

MAKAYLA. So why are we here? Are you having a breakdown?

CHLOE. Well I'm not happy of course. But you all know me and know nothing can keep me down.

SARAH. Well, there was that time when you were like moody all summer because your parents grounded you for sneaking out of the house.

CHLOE. I was a kid then.

LAUREN. That was last year.

CHLOE. Enough. I called you here because I want to start my own cheerleading squad.

MAKAYLA. What? That's insane. They're not going to let TWO SQUADS cheer during games.

CHLOE. Not sports. Scholastics! We will be the Scholastic Cheer Squad. They don't have one and it's never been done. So pioneer of us!

SARAH. There's a reason it hasn't been done. It's stupid.

LAUREN. Maybe not. I mean Chloe and I have the moves down.

CHLOE. And we can make up some total new ones.

MAKAYLA. What are we gonna do…cheer kids who get great report cards?

CHLOE. I found out the scholastic club is going to compete in a bunch of quiz bowls this year. And we'll be right on the sidelines to cheer them on.

SARAH. I can see it now. Give me an E give me an M give me a C-SQUARED...what's that spell? Einstein's formula! Go, team!

CHLOE. I'm serious here. Why should we waste two years of valuable cheerleading experience just because we didn't win the popularity contest...and we all know that's how they choose cheerleaders.

MAKAYLA. Hey, I'm popular!

LAUREN. Yeah, but your parents are poor so money is a factor. *(Quickly.)* But they're really good people and hard workers so...

CHLOE. Mrs. Esswein is totally on board with this. She's the faculty advisor for the scholastic club so what she says, goes.

LAUREN. I'm in!

SARAH. Heck, why not? Sure. I could use the exercise.

(They all look at MAKAYLA. She holds for a moment.)

MAKAYLA. Do we get uniforms?

CHLOE. The hottest ones money can buy...my mom already agreed to break out her American Express Black Card.

SARAH. Do you think the other cheerleaders will make fun of us?

CHLOE. We'll be so good they will be nothing but jealous.

MAKAYLA. I want color-coordinated pom-poms. And not cheap ones where they fall apart after one cheer.

CHLOE. Done and done!

*(**NATHAN,** a smart-looking boy in glasses, walks past. He carries a stack of books. The **GIRLS** all take note of him.)*

NATHAN, NATHAN...HE'S OUR MAN...

LAUREN, SARAH & MAKAYLA. IF NATHAN CAN'T DO IT NOBODY CAN!

*(**NATHAN** is a bit spooked by that and heads off quickly. They follow him.)*

CHLOE, SARAH, MAKAYLA & LAUREN. NATHAN, NATHAN, HE'S OUR MAN...IF HE CAN'T DO IT NOBODY CAN. NATHAN, NATHAN...

(They are gone.)

Scene Nine

(LILLIAN sits on a cube, writing on a yellow legal pad. AUBREY and JOSE approach.)

JOSE. Do you ever stop working on homework, Lillian?

AUBREY. Yeah, take a break already.

LILLIAN. I'm not doing homework.

JOSE. Then why else you using old-school paper and pen?

AUBREY. *(Mocking.)* Practicing your cursive?

LILLIAN. I'm making a bucket list.

AUBREY. I think you got like at least another seventy years before you have to think about that.

LILLIAN. A lot of kids do these…you don't have to be old to list stuff you dare yourself to do.

JOSE. Are you sick or something?

LILLIAN. I'm fine. This is my middle school bucket list… things I want to do before I make the jump to high school.

AUBREY. Jumping to high school IS my bucket list. Can't wait to get out of here.

LILLIAN. Well I'm here for another year and I want to make the most of it.

JOSE. So what do you have on the list?

LILLIAN. Not much so far. A few things.

AUBREY. Like…?

LILLIAN. Skipping class.

JOSE. Been there. Done that. Many times.

AUBREY. That's because you're a juvenile delinquent. Ha-ha. Lillian is too much of a good girl to do that.

LILLIAN. Whatever that means.

(Beat.)

I also want to get cast in the school play.

JOSE. The drama club is having auditions for *Peter Pan* next week.

LILLIAN. I know.

JOSE. My bucket list would include dating Kimberly Hunter. So hot!

LILLIAN. I'm only choosing bucket list things that I actually have a shot at.

> (**LILLIAN** and **AUBREY** *laugh.*)

AUBREY. What else you got?

LILLIAN. Getting switched out of Mr. Richards' English class.

JOSE. Why would you do that? Dude is so easy…all he does is show movies all day.

LILLIAN. Some of us actually want to learn something.

AUBREY. Hey I'll trade you.

LILLIAN. And at the very top of my list is "Being a Female Rapper."

JOSE. Get out of here, you?

LILLIAN. What does that mean?

JOSE. You're like the poster child for "NOT a female rapper."

AUBREY. Yeah, where's that coming from?

> (**LILLIAN** *pulls a big file folder from her backpack.*)

LILLIAN. From like a file of over 100 of my poems that I turned into rap songs. I spit them in my bedroom but I want to do it publicly.

AUBREY. You "spit" them? Wow. Just when you think you know someone.

LILLIAN. I'm serious!

AUBREY. Hey, I got a good rap name for you, Straight A!

LILLIAN. I love that!

> (*They hear a bell.*)

AUBREY. Oh man, this lunch went way too fast.

LILLIAN. They always do.

JOSE. I got an idea…you want to cross one of those things off your list?

AUBREY. Skipping out.

LILLIAN. Now?

JOSE. We can go over to my place. I got some great beat tracks. Lillian can try out a couple of her songs on us?

AUBREY. Yeah, start with a small audience and work your way up.

> (**LILLIAN** *thinks for a moment. She then takes her pen and dramatically crosses something off her list.*)

LILLIAN. Done and done. Now let's not just skip, when we can run!

> *(They exit.)*

Scene Ten

*(**ANDREA** enters and holds a couple of birthday balloons.)*

ANDREA. Today is my thirteenth birthday. Just five years younger than the age when my mom gave birth to me. I kind of wanted to just go out with my friends tonight but my mom insists that I celebrate it with her. Don't get me wrong, I love my mom, but she's starting to worry me. She told me last week how it's so "awesome" that I'm finally a teenager because since she still feels like a teenager we can be "besties"...does anybody even use those words anymore? She even wants to watch her favorite movie *Freaky Friday* tonight. That's the movie where the mother and daughter switch bodies and live each other's life. That's not freaky, that's creepy! My mom would so not fit in at this school. I have a hard enough time and I'm the same age as everyone. I think part of my mom's problem is that after she turned thirty, and she and my dad got divorced, she felt unwanted and old. She started dressing like a teenager and it's silly. I just want to shake her and say, "You are beautiful the way you are and I don't want you to be my friend, I need you to be my MOM!" Well, maybe I can tell her that sometime without the shaking part. So, happy birthday to me and I just hope if my mom buys me clothes as a present she doesn't buy herself a matching outfit.

(She exits.)

Scene Eleven

*(**GABRIELLA** stands at her locker talking to **BENJAMIN**. He sees what she doesn't. Coming toward them is **CLAIRE**, followed by her "followers," **BROOKLYN**, **SAVANNAH**, and **THOMAS**.)*

BENJAMIN. Oh, no, here comes your queen. Prepare to bow...

GABRIELLA. Benny, stop. You're just jealous.

*(**CLAIRE** has arrived. She exchanges disapproving looks with **BENJAMIN**, followed by her three **FOLLOWERS** doing the same to him.)*

CLAIRE. We have business to discuss with Gaby. You can leave...

BENJAMIN. And you can...

GABRIELLA. *(Cutting him off.)* Benny, I'll catch up with you later.

BENJAMIN. *(Parting shot to **CLAIRE**.)* Her name is Gabriella, not Gaby.

*(**BENJAMIN** exits.)*

CLAIRE. Today is your lucky day. I have an opening in my crew. It includes all the perks, like invites to my parties, weekend stayovers at my fabulous house, and of course a big spike in your social standing at this school because you would be associated with me. Interested?

GABRIELLA. Well, you do have great parties and...

CLAIRE. *(Cutting her off.)* Fine. Before you can be accepted you have to take a simple initiation test.

GABRIELLA. Test?

CLAIRE. Four multiple choice questions. I ask the question... *(Points to her crew.)* they offer you choices...and you must pick the right one. Ready?

GABRIELLA. Well, I...

CLAIRE. Number one: You're at one of my parties and you see someone there not on the invite list. What do you do?

BROOKLYN. A: Find Claire immediately and tell her.

SAVANNAH. B: Deal with it yourself and escort the loser out.

THOMAS. C: Nothing.

GABRIELLA. Well, I guess B because I wouldn't want to bother Claire?

CLAIRE. Correct. Number two: I send you a text at night explaining I was binge-watching Netflix and couldn't write a paper I was assigned for history class. What do you text back?

BROOKLYN. A: You'll meet Claire at school early the next day to help her write it.

SAVANNAH. B: Ask her to text you what the subject of the assignment is and write it for her.

THOMAS. C: Tell her you're still doing your own homework and you can't help her.

GABRIELLA. B?

CLAIRE. Of course.

   (Beat.)

Number three: We're both wearing the same outfit at school. Your choices...

BROOKLYN. A: Ask Claire what she wants you to do.

SAVANNAH. B: You go home immediately and change.

THOMAS. C: It would never happen because Claire is too cutting-edge fashionable for anyone at this school to wear what she is wearing.

GABRIELLA. *(Starting to think this is absurd.)* C?

CLAIRE. Correct. And now the final question. Get it right and you're in. Number four: You have a friend that I don't like, for instance that loser Benjamin you hang out with. I ask you to dump him as a friend. What's the first thing you say?

BROOKLYN. A: Let me think about it.

SAVANNAH. B: I feel sorry for him, please reconsider your request.

THOMAS. C: Kick that lame-o to the curb!

> (**GABRIELLA** *thinks about it for a moment. Smiles.*)

GABRIELLA. D. I would tell you that I must have been crazy to want to hang out with someone as self-centered, rude, and shallow as you. I would then tell you to get out of my face and then I'd go spend the rest of the day with my best friend ever, Benjamin, who likes his real friends to call him Benny.

> (*Pause, enjoying* **CLAIRE***'s shock.*)

Don't let my locker door hit you on your big fat –

> (*Beat.*)

mouth.

> (**GABRIELLA** *slams the locker and exits.*)

THOMAS. D? We didn't offer her a D...did we?

> (**CLAIRE** *is fuming. She turns and exits in the other direction.* **BROOKLYN, SAVANNAH,** *and* **THOMAS** *hurry after her.*)

Scene Twelve

*(**WYATT** enters wearing a jacket and carrying his backpack. His phone rings.)*

WYATT. I'll be out in a minute.

(Pause.)

Yeah. Okay.

(Hangs up. Notices audience.)

Most kids would be glad to get out of school early on Monday. I would too, but not for this. My parents got a divorce and they are convinced I'll be so screwed up because of it that they make me go to a shrink. Well, I'm not happy about their divorce for sure, but I don't really need a professional anything to help me deal with it. They still think I'm like ten years old or something. That's about the time I started to notice it. My dad coming home later. My mom crying so much. The both of them arguing all the time.

(Beat.)

All the time. I knew where that was headed. So I've had plenty of time to get ready for it. I tried my best to keep them together. For a while I studied my butt off to try to get really good grades. I thought if I showed them I was doing well in school they'd be proud of what they created together. I know it sounds crazy and of course that didn't work. So every Monday my mom picks me up and drives me to Dr. Handley's office where we talk for one very expensive hour. Actually he does most of the talking. Not sure how much longer I'll have to see him but I coulda told him the very first appointment that I don't need to talk about it with him or anybody else. What I need is for my mom and dad to get back together and be the family that we're supposed to be.

(His phone rings again. He looks at who is calling and then exits.)

Scene Thirteen

> (**DAVID** *enters and encourages a skeptical* **BRIANNE** *to follow.*)

DAVID. Come on...

BRIANNE. Are you sure this is okay?

DAVID. Mr. Lemkin gave me the key.

BRIANNE. But these driving simulators are for high school kids. They just keep them here because our school has more room.

DAVID. Our turf. We should get to use them. Besides we'll be in high school next year...and driving before you know it.

BRIANNE. I don't know...

DAVID. Come on, it'll be fun.

> (*They cross to two cubes that are next to each other.* **DAVID** *acts likes he's climbing into the simulator.*)

Get in.

> (**BRIANNE** *squeezes in next to him.*)

BRIANNE. Why do you get to drive?

DAVID. 'Cause I'm the man.

BRIANNE. No you're still just a boy. And it sounds like something my grandpa would say...right before Grandma sets him straight about women being equal.

DAVID. Just kidding. You can drive...

> (*They switch places.*)

BRIANNE. So this thing is kinda like virtual reality, right?

DAVID. Yeah. Here, put these on.

> (**DAVID** *hands her some VR goggles and then puts a pair on himself. He pushes a button and we hear the sound of the device turning on.*)

These things are much better than the old antique simulators the school used to use. These suckers are state of the art. You'll really *feel* the driving experience.

BRIANNE. Why don't we just drive a real car?

DAVID. 'Cause we're not old enough yet. But this will be good practice.

Just step on the gas when you're ready to go.

BRIANNE. I thought these were electric.

DAVID. Hybrid.

> (**BRIANNE** *puts her hands on an imaginary wheel; they both react as if the car lurches forward and they're driving fast.*)
>
> (*As they drive we hear race-car-type sound effects.*)

BRIANNE. Whoa...this is wild!

DAVID. Isn't this realistic? Like we're really in a car, cruisin' down the highway?

BRIANNE. It is real. I can actually feel the wind on my face.

DAVID. Left turn...

> (*She turns the wheel to the left. They both lean to the left.*)

Right turn...

> (*They lean to the right.*)

Steep hill ahead.

> (*They lean back.*)

And down the hill...

> (*They lean forward.*)

BRIANNE. Oh my god, it's raining

DAVID. Hey, it simulates ALL driving conditions. Isn't this great!

BRIANNE. This is fun. I'm driving!

> (**DAVID** *mimes pushing a button on the console. We hear a warning indicator sound.*)

DAVID. *(Smiling.)* Uh-oh...

BRIANNE. What's that? What's wrong? We're slowing down. What's happening?

DAVID. We've run out of gas.

BRIANNE. Run out of gas? Can't we switch to battery-powered?

DAVID. Uh...we ran out of that, too?

BRIANNE. What?

DAVID. Oh look...we've stopped on a hill that overlooks the city. How romantic!

> (**DAVID** *squirts some breath spray into his mouth, then starts to put his arm around* **BRIANNE.** *She takes off her goggles and pushes him off.* **DAVID** *takes off his goggles.*)

BRIANNE. I'm so sure. What do you think you're doing?

DAVID. Part of the "total" realistic experience.

BRIANNE. You had this planned all along.

DAVID. Well...

BRIANNE. I don't believe this. You cretin!

> (**BRIANNE** *punches his arm, then gets out and exits.*)

Now that's the kind of "real" you'll be seeing a lot of if you ever do talk a girl into actually dating you!

DAVID. *(Rubs his arm, gets out of the simulator.)* Brianne, wait up. Brianne...we can take Uber for our second date.

> *(He exits.)*

Scene Fourteen

*(**ANTHONY** enters, about to do another video selfie. Holds his phone up in front of his face.)*

ANTHONY. *(To camera.)* Friday, October thirtieth, 9:45 a.m. Bus had a flat tire so anyone riding on it was excused for missing their first two classes. Some days instead of broccoli, life serves you a nice round glazed donut... that's wonderfully flat on one side.

*(**ANTHONY** exits.)*

Scene Fifteen

*(We see two flashlights in the darkness. As they approach, the stage lights come up just a bit to reveal **NICHOLAS** and **MICHAEL**.)*

MICHAEL. Let's get out of here…this place is bad enough during the day.

NICHOLAS. Relax no one is here.

MICHAEL. But there are cameras and we broke in. Hard to "relax."

NICHOLAS. I'm not worried.

MICHAEL. I can't believe you talked me into this. And you didn't even take your phone back!

NICHOLAS. I told you I just wanted to delete some pictures on it. If I would have taken it from Mrs. Garrison's desk she would know it was me.

MICHAEL. She took it from you, sounds fair to me that you'd take it back.

NICHOLAS. Doesn't work that way.

MICHAEL. Do you really think she would have looked through your pics?

NICHOLAS. I couldn't take that chance. And you should be happy too because I deleted the one of you smoking a cigarette.

MICHAEL. That was a gag picture. I didn't smoke it.

NICHOLAS. She doesn't know that. Or that a lot of the photos are just staged. My parents would never believe me that they're fake or that…

(Suddenly, they hear an alarm.)

MICHAEL. Oh no, we're busted. I hate you…

NICHOLAS. You don't think I thought this might happen. I got a plan. Follow me.

*(**NICHOLAS** heads stage right.)*

MICHAEL. Where you going?

NICHOLAS. To the library.

MICHAEL. That's right, the library has a door to the outside.

(Beat.)

I'm pretty sure that'll be locked too...on both sides.

NICHOLAS. I think I can open it.

MICHAEL. What if you can't?

NICHOLAS. My plan has a backup plan. If we can't get out the door, we'll stay in the library.

MICHAEL. What?!

NICHOLAS. It's genius. You see, we tell them that we broke in to use the library...to STUDY. Who is going to be mad at us for that? Can you see the headlines: "Two Students Were Arrested in the School Library for Trying to Learn Stuff."

MICHAEL. I don't know...

NICHOLAS. We'll record it and it will go viral. We'll be stars!

MICHAEL. You sure about this?

NICHOLAS. The library is like a church...it's a sanctuary...all are welcome...all are safe...no judgments.

MICHAEL. I don't know about this.

NICHOLAS. Do what you want. But I have faith in my plan.

> *(**NICHOLAS** exits. **MICHAEL** isn't sure he wants to follow, but does so when he hears the alarm stop and voices in the distance.)*

Scene Sixteen

> (**HAILEY** *enters and looks around nervously. She turns and is startled to see the audience, but then realizes who it is.*)

HAILEY. Scared me there for a minute. I thought you were students. I have to be careful because I can't risk any of the kids here seeing me with...this.

> (*She turns around and reveals she is wearing a* Sesame Street *backpack.*)

Can you believe this? My mom bought it for me last week for my birthday. *Sesame Street*? Seriously? I stopped watching that when I was like seven years old which is obviously the age she still thinks I am. It comes from her own fear of getting older and losing me as her little angel. Angel? If she only knew how un-angelic I really am. Since she picks me up after school every day, I have to sneak out of here with this grotesque and childish thing strapped to my back like some kind of baby turtle clamoring its way back to the safety of the open sea. The rest of the time it's in a double paper bag in my double-locked locker. It's only been a week that I've played this hide-and-geek game, but I'm getting real tired of it. I would just tell her that I think it's stupid and it embarrasses me but my mother is very fragile. It would be like a big tear-fest and then I'd feel guilty for the rest of my life so I have to figure out another way to deal with this. At first I was going to toss it in the trash and tell her it was stolen, but she would just buy me another one. Scratch that idea. So until I come up with another plan I have to do it this way. Maybe I could stick it in another backpack so that...

> (*She spots other* **STUDENTS** *coming her way.*)

GIRL STUDENT #1. Hailey, wait up...

HAILEY. Oh, I can't. Mom's waiting. Call me later!

> (**HAILEY** *walks backwards fast so they can't see the backpack as she makes an exit.*)

Scene Seventeen

*(Four **STUDENTS** enter walking in almost military-march-like formation. We don't see their faces at first because they are buried in books. When they reach the center they turn and face the audience and then lower their books to reveal their faces. They all wear glasses.)*

STUDENT #1. We are the bright and serious students.

STUDENT #2. We are the future scholars.

STUDENT #3. We love to study.

STUDENT #4. We love homework.

STUDENT #1. We love books!

(They all sigh happily in unison.)

We've been waiting for middle school for many years.

STUDENT #2. Because here, knowledge is strength.

STUDENT #3. Because here, learning is a good thing.

STUDENT #4. The classes are more challenging.

STUDENT #2. The homework is harder.

STUDENT #1. And having a big brain is sexier.

*(The other three give **STUDENT #1** a look on that.)*

STUDENT #4. Most important, the library is bigger and better and bookier.

STUDENT #2. And even though we all are fully aware that "bookier" isn't a word, it sums up who we are...

STUDENT #3. What we do...

STUDENT #1. And where we put our priorities.

STUDENT #4. While the other students complain about homework...

STUDENT #1. We embrace it. Give us more!

STUDENT #2. While the others worry more about their social standing...

STUDENT #3. It means nothing, because we have each other.

STUDENT #4. Call us brainiacs.

STUDENT #2. Call us eggheads.

STUDENT #1. Call us nerds.

STUDENT #2. But be forewarned, we will fight back in our own way.

STUDENT #3. We'll tell the teachers they should assign more homework.

STUDENT #1. We'll stop you from copying off our papers.

STUDENT #4. We'll show your parents our report cards.

STUDENT #2. And we'll raise the bar so high that you will only be able to walk under it.

ALL. You have no idea who you're messing with!

STUDENT #3. We are not just the A team, we are the Straight A team!

STUDENT #1. We are the serious students.

STUDENT #2. We are the future scholars.

STUDENT #3. We love books.

STUDENT #4. We love homework.

STUDENT #1. We love to study.

ALL. And someday we will rule the world!

> *(Books back up to cover their faces as they march off in single file like they marched on.)*

Scene Eighteen

(**CHRISTINA** *enters.*)

CHRISTINA. I'd really like to know at what point I totally lost my popularity. In first grade through fifth grade I was the most popular kid ever. Everybody wanted to be with me. My birthday parties had standing room only. My Valentine's Day box overflowed with cards. Even though we were all too young to date I had more boys around me than I could count. So what happened? I noticed it about halfway through sixth grade. No particular day. Just woke up one day and started to realize that there was a real Christina chill in the air when I'd walk down the hall. The girls who used to be my bests were now so distant. The boys who used to want to hang out with me suddenly seemed to avoid eye contact. Everybody just seemed so unfriendly. So cold.

(Beat.)

It hurts. A lot. I am still me... I haven't changed. Maybe that was the reason. Everybody else has changed and I stayed right where I was. I thought when I got here to this school I'd be even more popular. But it's just the opposite. Nobody is mean to me or anything; they just don't seem to want to be my friend anymore. I'm not giving up because it could be a temporary thing. I hope it's just a temporary thing. Maybe high school will be different. Maybe by then I'll be different and they'll want back on the Christina train. I just don't understand this... I just don't understand what I did wrong?

(She exits.)

Scene Nineteen

(REBECCA walks down the hall. Out of nowhere springs ERIC. He wears some sort of official hat. REBECCA screams and then sees who it is.)

REBECCA. Jeez, give me a heart attack already!

ERIC. Where you headed?

REBECCA. What do you care?

ERIC. I'll ask you again. Where are you headed?

REBECCA. Back off, Eric. I don't need this today.

ERIC. Just doing my duty and you know it.

REBECCA. Oh please, you're just being your usual annoying self.

(Notices.) And what is that thing on your head.

ERIC. My ISSO hat?

REBECCA. ISSO?

ERIC. Intra School Security Officer.

REBECCA. OMG! That is so stupid. You're a hall monitor. Inflate your importance much?

ERIC. You don't bother me, rule-breaker.

REBECCA. More like a fool-breaker. Because I busted you for being the pretend patrol!

ERIC. Enough of this. Show me your pass.

REBECCA. Yeah, enough of this is right. I'm your sister for Pete's sake.

ERIC. Rules apply to all. Blood relatives included.

REBECCA. You are so lame.

ERIC. In other words you don't have a pass? You are aware of the penalties for that, aren't you? *(Before she can answer.)* Probably not, so let me tell you: Code 432, Section 3A. "Failure to present authorized documentation while travelling in a school hallway during scheduled class time." Comes with a possible penalty of two to five days of detention.

REBECCA. You're losing it, Eric.

ERIC. I'm doing my job, ma'am.

REBECCA. Ma'am. You're one year older than me and you called me ma'am?

ERIC. I'll ask you one last time. Where are you headed?

REBECCA. I'm going to the restroom.

ERIC. I don't see Mr. Anderson's hall pass.

REBECCA. I'm not lugging that big stupid steering wheel thingy around. He said I could go.

ERIC. And I'm supposed to take your word for it?

REBECCA. I don't care what you take… I'm going to the bathroom.

(She starts to walk past him, he blocks her way.)

ERIC. Don't make me call backup!

REBECCA. Backup? I'm gonna tell Mom you've been watching too many cop shows. Look, I'm "backed up" and unless you want an accident right here on the floor I suggest you get out of my face and out of my way.

ERIC. No can do, missy.

REBECCA. Let me put it another way. You move or I will tell everyone you know that you still sleep every night with your teddy bear Yogi.

ERIC. You wouldn't.

REBECCA. See how serious people take you after that!

*(**ERIC** thinks about that. Takes out a small notepad. Writes something down, hands it to her.)*

ERIC. This is an official but temporary hall pass. Good for one trip. I am authorized to issue this.

REBECCA. You are so full of yourself.

(She takes the paper and exits down the hall.)

ERIC. And I'm timing you!

*(He sees a **STUDENT** walk past him and reacts.)*

Freeze!

*(The **STUDENT** panics a bit and runs away. **ERIC** gives chase.)*

ERIC. Pull it over, Chamberlin!

(They're gone.)

Scene Twenty

(**DANIEL** *enters. He is dressed in a Peter Pan costume.*)

DANIEL. Before you jump to conclusions here, this is a costume. I don't want you to think I dress like this for school or anything, although it might be fun to do that. I'm playing Peter Pan in the school play. It's not the usual kind of production as Mr. Rowlands wrote it himself and it's a little different than the original story. I've wanted to be an actor ever since I can remember. My first part was in second grade when I played a carrot...that's right a carrot. Don't ask. But I remember how excited I was when the audience applauded me. I was hooked. Right then I knew what I wanted to be. One person who won't be seeing me perform tonight is my dad. He thinks theater is a waste of time. He loves coming to see me play sports. That's what he wants for me but doesn't seem to care what I want for me. I played football and basketball but I decided that was enough and auditioned for the play. I beat out ten other guys for this part. I love my dad, but he just doesn't get it. He just doesn't get me. I told him I'm not giving up sports but the truth is I'm not giving up acting. The high school does three plays a year and I intend on trying out for all of them. Peter Pan doesn't want to grow up, but I do. And when I do I am going to be the greatest actor ever.

(**JENNIFER** *enters.*)

JENNIFER. Five minutes until curtain, Daniel.
DANIEL. Okay.

(**JENNIFER** *exits.*)

I hear we have a full house tonight. It would be great if one of the people in the audience was my dad. Even though he wouldn't admit it, I think he'd be impressed.

(**DANIEL** *exits.*)

Scene Twenty-One

> (**PAULA** *enters. She is holding a wireless microphone in one hand and a notecard in the other hand.*)

PAULA. Okay, here's a good spot. Let's go...we've got to be set up before classes are dismissed.

> (**ETHAN** *enters, followed by* **JACK**. **ETHAN** *is carrying a hand-held camera.*)

ETHAN. Nothing to set up. I'm ready to roll.

JACK. What did you want me to do again?

PAULA. You're the bouncer. Anybody acts like an idiot or gets in my face it's your job to get them out of here. Crack heads if you have to.

JACK. I'm not crackin' anybody's head, Paula.

PAULA. I didn't mean literally.

ETHAN. The light's better if you stand in the center.

PAULA. Let me do the cold open first and we can then jump edit right to the interviews when we get them.

ETHAN. I'm ready...in five–four–three–two...

PAULA. Welcome to another edition of *Middle School TV*'s most favorite segment, "Paula in the Hall-a" starring me, Paula Logan. We're going to be asking students what they think of a number of issues facing us here in this inist...stitution.
(*To* **ETHAN**.) Keep rolling.
(*To camera.*) ...Issues facing us here in this school.

> (*We hear a bell.*)

> (*Some* **STUDENTS** *enter and they spot* **PAULA**. *A couple of them avoid her like the plague but...*)

Maya...over here!

> (**MAYA** *reluctantly crosses to her as more* **STUDENTS** *enter. Some watch, others exit.*)

We're asking students today what they think of school so far this year. What do you think has been the best part of being here?

MAYA. Well, for me, certainly all my friends. It's different than when we were together in elementary...

PAULA. *(Cutting her off.)* I mean what is your biggest gripe so far about being here.

MAYA. I don't really have gripe. So far it's been...

PAULA. *(To camera.)* Okay, well let's see what others have to say.

> *(PAULA motions for JACK to clear MAYA out of the way. As he does, PAULA waves over CAMERON, who is standing with several other STUDENTS who are waiting to be interviewed.)*

What is your biggest gripe about this school?

CAMERON. Yeah I got one. Food. The cafeteria is the worst ever. Yesterday whatever they put on my plate started moving and I had to defend myself with a fork. And the vegetables looked like a bunch of boogers.

> *(He laughs hard at his own joke and PAULA rolls her eyes. JACK is back and drags CAMERON out of there.)*

PAULA. Next.

> *(LAURA crosses to her.)*

Help me out here, Laura.

LAURA. I do have a gripe. Homework.

> *(She is emboldened by other STUDENTS voicing their agreement.)*

PAULA. Tell it, sister!

LAURA. *(Her intensity builds through this.)* The amount of homework here should not take us longer to do than the amount of time we spend here during the day. When do we have time to sleep or do anything else with our lives? School shouldn't just be about homework. Teachers don't realize that a major important part of learning doesn't take place in the classroom. It's out here in the halls, in the parking lot, in the cafeteria, in the gym and all the other places where we learn to be who we are meant to be. We need to develop the social skills we will use our entire lives. Those skills are more important than math, science, and English combined. Stop the homework. Lighten our loads. Set us free!

*(The **STUDENTS** all applaud.)*

PAULA. *(To camera.)* There you have it viewers. Too much homework. Join us next time when we put our finger on the pulse of this school and bring it to you mostly live. Right here on the number-one middle school TV network in the state and right here on "Paula in the Hall-a"!

ETHAN. Is that a wrap?

PAULA. *(Sarcastic.)* No, we need to get Jack on camera.

JACK. Really?

PAULA. No, not really.

*(To **ETHAN**.)* This is our best one yet…let's hit the editing room.

*(**ETHAN** and **PAULA** exit. **JACK** stays for a moment.)*

JACK. I'd like to be on camera sometime.

*(**JACK** exits.)*

Scene Twenty-Two

(**VICTOR** *enters.*)

VICTOR. Wanna hear a joke? Knock-knock. Who's there? My pancreas. My pancreas who? My pancreas that hasn't worked since I was three years old.

*(We hear collective **STUDENT** groans and boos from offstage.)*

Not really funny, but true. They know what I'm talking about. My name is Victor and I'm a T1. No, not something from *The Terminator* although wearing an insulin pump makes me part cyborg. I've had Type 1 diabetes as long as I can remember. Since I've had this disease so long it's just a natural part of my life and although it's something I have to think about 24/7 I've learned to live with it and control it...even though some days it does seem to control me. I also learned a long time ago that everybody has something in life that they struggle with so I'm not going to whine about my thing. But what does bother me is that even though tens of millions of people on the planet have diabetes; so many people I meet still don't understand it. First of all, you don't get it by eating sugar. Period. That's an old myth. And also there are two main types: Type 1 like me which means I need to inject insulin because my pancreas doesn't make any; or Type 2 which means that someone makes insulin but their bodies don't use it right. Okay I'll end the lecture there but if people would just know those two simple things then people like me would be a whole lot better off. My friends are cool and they get it, maybe because I've told them a gazillion times. Oh, and just because I have diabetes it doesn't mean I can't do what any other kids my age can do. Like sports. Or music. Or anything. Even though there are some bad complications to having diabetes one of the good complications is that it makes people who have it incredibly sexy. Okay, I made that one up, but it's okay to spread that myth everywhere, especially here at this school!

    (**VICTOR** *exits.*)

Scene Twenty-Three

(**JENNA**, **FRANKLIN**, **SOPHIE**, *and* **ABIGAIL** *sit on cubes in a semi-circle while* **SAVANNAH** *paces back and forth.*)

SAVANNAH. Come on gang, this thing is due on Thursday and we need to ALL work together to come up with something.

JENNA. Maybe we can get an extension.

SAVANNAH. Not gonna happen. Mr. Warren doesn't budge on deadlines. You know that?

FRANKLIN. I still think that my idea was the best.

ABIGAIL. Don't start with that again. Nobody is going to use an app that reminds them to take a shower.

SOPHIE. Yeah, if you need something like that then it's okay if you smell because you're too dumb to have friends.

SAVANNAH. Part of this design-an-app assignment thing was to work as a group. And some of you haven't offered anything...JENNA!

JENNA. Okay, I do have something. I call it the TEST PREDICTOR.

FRANKLIN. Sounds interesting?

JENNA. You enter in as much information about a teacher as you can and it gives you a prediction on when they might spring a test on you so you're prepared.

SOPHIE. I like that.

SAVANNAH. Not bad, but the app is supposed to be for the students not about a teacher. Mr. Warren would never go for that.

ABIGAIL. We should definitely do that on our own...you know later.

FRANKLIN. How about an app like WebMD that tells you things you can say you have that will get you out of taking showers in gym class.

SOPHIE. What's this obsession you have with showers, Franklin?

JENNA. Yeah, that's really weird?

SAVANNAH. Okay, you people are lucky because I thought of something last night that would be like perf. The "Homework Friend"!

ABIGAIL. Please tell me it's an app that does homework for us!

SOPHIE. I'd be for that.

FRANKLIN. Sign me up!

SAVANNAH. In your dreams. No this is more practical. It's like Facebook only it pairs you up with other kids who are good in a subject you're not. For instance Jenna is a math whiz but not so good at Spanish like Sophie. So the app pulls in your classmates who are good at a subject, factors in if you're friends on Facebook and bingo, you have a match with someone who can help you.

SOPHIE. I think there's already something like that.

SAVANNAH. This is different because it's only for kids in this middle school. People you know and might not know, but we already have the data in the school computer about what they get good grades in.

JENNA. I like it. And we can also streamline it so you're paired up with someone who is weak in what you do and strong in what you're weak in so you can really help each other.

FRANKLIN. And also include how often they take a shower so you can tell if you want to meet up on the phone instead of in person.

(The GIRLS all look at him.)

I'm kidding, jeez.

SAVANNAH. Are we all in agreement about the "Homework Friend" app?

ABIGAIL. I think it needs a better name.

JENNA. How about "Two by Two"?

FRANKLIN. Sounds like Noah's Ark.

SOPHIE. How about "Study Peeps"?

SAVANNAH. Sounds like an Easter treat.

(**JENNA** *looks up something on her iPad.*)

JENNA. I got it…"Homie Work"…it's in the Urban Dictionary but it's not an app.

SAVANNAH. Well it is now. Okay, gang. We have our project. Jenna you talk to the front office about the school computer.

JENNA. They'll never let me use that.

SAVANNAH. You don't have to; just gather some facts that we can list on how it could be used.

SOPHIE. I'll do a poll thingy to ask other kids how many would use something like this.

ABIGAIL. And I'll draw up a design for the app!

FRANKLIN. What should I do?

SAVANNAH. Go home and take a shower.

(*They all laugh.*)

You can help Sophie with the poll.

(*To all.*) Let's roll, gang. We're like all going to get an A on this.

(*They exit.*)

Scene Twenty-Four

>*(**NATHAN** enters playing a portable video game. He stops to take a paperback book out of his backpack.)*

NATHAN. My grandpa gave me this book for my birthday. He does that every year. It would be nice if one year he'd give me some money to buy what I really want. Don't get me wrong, I love my gramps but the dude is really old school. He's always complaining that kids today don't have an imagination because we're always playing video games. He's a real "get off my lawn" type of old guy. That's okay, he may not get us but I get him. And he's wrong about young people today. We do have an imagination; it's just different than his generation had. We're always just one click away from going anywhere in the world. We can see videos of things that in his day they could only read about. And we do read a lot, just not always in the pages of books. Our reading is on a screen, but it's still reading. For instance, this book he gave me, *The Adventures of Tom Sawyer* by Mark Twain…I didn't have the heart to tell him I already read it…as an eBook! Grandma and I plan a little surprise for him on his next birthday. We're going to get him a Virtual Reality headset. I can't wait to see the look on his face when he experiences that for the first time. It's so real he might even start shouting "Get off my lawn!" at the digital images he sees.

>*(He puts the book back in his bag and continues with his video game as he exits.)*

Scene Twenty-Five

> (**ALANA** *enters the stage and is followed by* **SIENA, SADIE, MARIA, CODY,** *and* **NOLAN.**)

ALANA. *(To the five students.)* Places please.

> *(They each sit on a cube.* **ALANA** *crosses downstage center and speaks to the audience.)*

The Detention Monologues...a very short stage play by Alana Slater. That would be me.

> (**ALANA** *crosses stage right and takes a spectator view of the group.* **CODY** *stands and crosses to center stage.*)

CODY. I admit I knew better than to be listening to my radio in class. But the *[local Major League baseball team]* had an afternoon game and I just had to know the score. I mean in this case I think them making the playoffs was a heck of a lot more important than learning about World War I. I never would have been caught if they didn't hit a grand slam in the ninth inning to blow the game wide open. How am I supposed to not scream when that happens? A grand slam! I may have lost my radio because of that...but my team won. Detention!

> (**CODY** *sits back down.* **SIENA** *is next.*)

SIENA. There's a lot of pressure on me because everyone else in my family is like so smart. My sister breezed through middle school with all As. Not even one B. I have to study like crazy just to get a B. My parents think I'm just as smart as her but lazy or something and mess around too much. My privileges are always on the line at report card time. So, yesterday when I heard that there was going to be a pop quiz in science class that I hadn't studied for, I had no choice but to pull the fire alarm. The other kids should thank me, because of my efforts nobody had to take that test. Detention!

> (**SIENA** *sits.* **SADIE** *is next.*)

SADIE. Who knew that Mr. Maxwell had no sense of humor about himself? If he wasn't so snoopy he never even would have seen that cartoon I drew of him. It was pretty darn good if I do say so myself. I drew him as a duck because he walks like one, has a big beak-like nose, and when he clears his throat he sounds just like a duck. Ack, ack, ack. Detention!

(SADIE sits. MARIA is next.)

MARIA. I was tardy. Again. Detention!

(MARIA sits. NOLAN is next.)

NOLAN. I held it in as long as I could. But I just can't handle sitting next to William, especially in a boring class because that guy can make you laugh just by looking at you. I sure did choose the wrong day for that because Mrs. Hoskins was all serious about something that happened in the news and was almost in tears. I tried to look away from William but it was too late. The laugh started throbbing in the bottom of my stomach and I could feel it working its way up to my mouth. I bit my lip to make it stop but the pain wasn't enough. And then it just came exploding out of me like the air out of a balloon when it pops!

(He recreates the laugh.)

To make matters worse, the whole class started laughing. I've never seen a face get as red as Mrs. Hoskins'. Detention!

(NOLAN crosses back to his cube. ALANA signals for all five of them to stand.)

ALL. Detention!

ALANA. The End.

(To audience.) This would be where you applaud!

(All five STUDENTS take a bow and then follow ALANA offstage.)

Scene Twenty-Six

*(**ANTHONY** enters to do another video selfie. Holds his phone up in front of his face.)*

ANTHONY. *(To camera.)* Tuesday, March sixth, 10:39 a.m. I want to publicly go on the record and say that I hate Braxton Caldwell.

(Beat.)

Okay, hate is too strong of a word...so I'll edit that to say I dislike, frowny face, and am really steamed at Braxton Caldwell. Since Mrs. Leslie grades on a curve his lone perfect score on the hardest test ever knocked my C down to a D. Thanks a lot, big booger brains!

(Lowers cell phone and exits.)

Scene Twenty-Seven

(DANNY enters. He looks around to make sure no one is there before talking to the audience.)

DANNY. Is it okay for a boy to ask out a girl if she's like a lot taller than he is? *(Quickly.)* Oh...uh...asking for a friend. Because I know this guy who is about my height and the girl he likes a lot is about five or six inches taller. I mean, that's a lot. It's not his fault because for some reason girls grow a lot faster than boys at this age. I'm sure I'll be taller... I mean he'll be taller than her in a few years, just not right now. I guess he could wear cowboy boots or something but if he does invite her to the dance in two weeks and she does accept, she might wear heels and then that completely wipes out what the boots would do for him. I told my friend that he should just go with his heart and not his height but you can see that this is awkward times infinity.

*(Just then he sees a tall **GIRL** walking hand-in-hand down the hall with a shorter **BOY**.)*

How weird is that? It's like they were listening or something. Or maybe it's a sign. Yeah, why do I even care about a few inches anyway? I'm going to ask Mallory out... I mean I better go tell my friend he should ask that tall girl he likes out.

(Heads off and stops, turns back to audience.)

Oh, and this is between us. What happens in middle school stays in middle school!

*(**DANNY** exits, never taking his eyes off the audience.)*

Scene Twenty-Eight

(CAROLINE and GENESIS enter stage left. MEGAN and BRIAN enter stage right. They all meet in the middle.)

GENESIS. Okay, this is how these negotiations are going to work. To avoid a big screaming match, I will speak for Caroline and Megan will speak for Brian. There will be no direct dialogue between the two warring parties.

MEGAN. They're not warring; they are simple having a little lovers' spat.

CAROLINE. *(To GENESIS.)* We're not lovers.

GENESIS. They are not lovers.

BRIAN. *(To MEGAN.)* After six months we're sure a lot more than friends.

MEGAN. Six months equals lovers in my book.

GENESIS. Caroline is totally mad that Brian was talking all during lunch with Paige instead of with her.

BRIAN. *(To MEGAN.)* Paige is my science partner. We're working on an assignment.

MEGAN. Jealous much. There is nothing to that. It's a working relationship, not a romantic one.

CAROLINE. *(To GENESIS.)* So they say.

GENESIS. She can see with her own eyes. And might I add that I personally know that Paige is about as bad at science as Brian is...so why weren't they each paired up with someone who could help them?

BRIAN. *(To MEGAN.)* I never complain when Caroline talks to Alex all the time.

MEGAN. *(To BRIAN.)* Yeah, but Alex is gay...and he's on the cheerleading squad with Caroline.

BRIAN. *(To MEGAN.)* Whose side are you on? Tell her...

MEGAN. *(Not convincing.)* Yeah, what about Alex?

CAROLINE. *(To GENESIS.)* Maybe Brian is jealous of me and has the hots for Alex.

GENESIS. Do you Brian?

BRIAN. No!

MEGAN. No!

CAROLINE. *(To GENESIS.)* I'm also mad because he forgot all about our six-month anniversary yesterday. And don't tell me he doesn't know it's six months he just said he knew.

GENESIS. Oh, Brian, that is a deal-breaker. Six months since your first date and you don't remember it?

MEGAN. *(To BRIAN.)* That's cold, bro.

BRIAN. *(To MEGAN.)* What? I do remember it. I DID remember it. I sent her flowers and one of those Build-A-Bear things...dressed in our school colors.

MEGAN. Awww. That's so sweet.

> *(CAROLINE pushes GENESIS out of the way.)*

CAROLINE. I didn't get anything.

> *(BRIAN pushes MEGAN out of the way. He takes out his cell phone.)*

BRIAN. I got a confirmation email that you did.
(Reads.) Says it was delivered yesterday at seven p.m.

CAROLINE. I was at cheerleading practice.

BRIAN. Somebody signed for them... *(Looks closer.)* Yeah, your brother Eddie!

CAROLINE. *(Grabs his phone. Looks at the confirmation.)* That little jerk. He is so toast.

BRIAN. I can't believe he didn't tell you.

CAROLINE. *(To BRIAN.)* I'm sorry for thinking you'd forget.

BRIAN. I can't blame you...you never got them. I wondered why you didn't call me. And I don't even like Paige. We really are working on a science project.

CAROLINE. I just said that because I was mad about yesterday. I'm so sorry.

> *(CAROLINE and BRIAN hug and exit holding hands.)*

GENESIS. *(To* **MEGAN.***)* Aww, a happy ending!

MEGAN. *(To* **GENESIS.***)* More like a successful negotiation… by skilled negotiators.

GENESIS. You're right.

> *(As they head off:)*

MEGAN. Hey, maybe we should offer our services to the Middle East problem…

GENESIS. Or at least my parents!

Scene Twenty-Nine

(**LUCAS** *enters.*)

LUCAS. My name is Lucas and there's nothing really special about that, but I'm going to tell you a little secret – my Twitter handle is ZORRO2THEMAX and I have over one hundred and fifty thousand followers. Many of the kids in this school and in our high school are fans of mine on Twitter and don't even know it. Some kids at this school call me Lucas the Loser and have fun picking on me – last week it was shoving me in a locker. It didn't bother me because I get the last laugh. You see, the same two guys who "lockered" me are followers who worship me online. Classic, right? I started ZORRO2THEMAX as a bit of a joke. An avatar that I can pretend to be some kind of living superhero guy. It took a while to get rolling, but I made him everything most guys fantasize about being – rich, studly, and a ladykiller. He is politically brilliant, hilariously witty, knows sports trivia and is a gourmet cook. Something for everybody. Men want to be like him. Women want to be with him...and little do any of those people know that he is a sixth-grader who sits at the lowlifes' table in the cafeteria. Do I feel bad about pretending to be something I am not? No way. Mr. Sheldon tells us that confidence is power. He spoke for a whole hour about "people want to believe in someone who is greater than they are." Hey, there is no one greater than ZORRO2THEMAX. He has mad skills! Besides, I know someday I will for real have the qualities that I pretend to have online. So I'm just borrowing from the future me.

(*Several* **STUDENTS** *walk by, including* **DYLAN**.)

DYLAN. Lucas the Loser!

(*The other* **STUDENTS** *laugh as the group exits.*)

LUCAS. That was Dylan. Last night he DM'd ZORRO2THEMAX asking him for advice on a girl he has a crush on. Even told me her name. What a dope. Now I know his secret. But he doesn't know mine. ZORRO2THEMAX for the win!

(**LUCAS** *exits...jubilantly.*)

Scene Thirty

*(**GRACE**, wearing a boy's jacket and tie, is talking to another **GIRL** who is also dressed in boys' clothes. **LAYLA** enters and spots her. She crosses to **GRACE** just as the other **GIRL** exits.)*

LAYLA. What's going on with you?

GRACE. About to head to math class...

LAYLA. You know what I'm talking about. What's with the Ken doll outfit?

GRACE. It's to support Sam.

LAYLA. You mean Sandy Metzger?

GRACE. Sandy now identifies as a boy and it's Sam now.

LAYLA. Yeah, I know. So does that mean that you're flipping too?

GRACE. Flipping? You mean do I no longer self-identify with the sex I was born with?

LAYLA. Whatever...you know what I mean.

GRACE. No, I'm still me as a girl. But today Sam and a few others are going to start getting names on a petition to present to the school board so they can use the restroom of the sex they associate themselves with.

LAYLA. Wow, sounds like something you memorized.

GRACE. It's something that I believe they should have the right to do.

LAYLA. Well not me.

GRACE. Obviously. But most of the kids I talk to don't care what others want to be. Besides, our bathroom breaks are so short anyway it really isn't an issue.

LAYLA. I think Sandy is just going through a phase.

GRACE. Sam.

(Beat.)

Maybe. Maybe not. We're all going through a lot of changes right now. Middle school is where we get a chance to sort things out.

LAYLA. Just seems so weird to me. Brenda is now Bobby. Jill is now Jack. So confusing!

GRACE. Well, it's not something that I'm planning on doing but I think we all should have the right to be who we want to be.

LAYLA. Well yeah, but...

(GRACE pulls out a clipboard.)

GRACE. Want to sign the petition.

LAYLA. Seriously?

GRACE. Yeah.

LAYLA. I don't know. I have to think about this.

GRACE. That's fine. You know something, that's what's great about middle school. We have opinions and choices now. And people are starting to let us make them for ourselves.

LAYLA. *(Thinks for a moment.)* Well, Sandy...I mean Sam is my neighbor. She...he's always been nice to me. I used to go with her family on vacation...I mean his family... whatever!

GRACE. Look I gotta go...

LAYLA. Wait.

(LAYLA grabs the clipboard and signs her name. Hands it back to GRACE.)

GRACE. Good choice...your choice!

LAYLA. Yeah, my choice.

(Beat.)

But there are two things I wonder about.

GRACE. What's that?

LAYLA. What my parents will say when I tell them I signed that.

GRACE. And?

LAYLA. When "Sam" uses the boys' restroom if he will leave the toilet seat up or down.

(They both share a laugh as they exit.)

Scene Thirty-One

(CYNTHIA enters and is not happy.)

CYNTHIA. Arrgghh! I'm so upset! I have to delete my Instagram account because of my mom. Oh it's not what you think. She liked what I was posting. She started following me! And then started "liking" every freakin' thing I posted. What good is being on social media if your mom is going to know everything you post, every comment you get and every person who follows you? I can't have any secrets, crushes, or even rants without her eyes all over it. There's only one thing left to do. Delete! So I deleted my account and created a new one. I lost all my pictures, all my followers, two years' worth of memories all because my mom wants to be part of my world. It doesn't work that way. Our worlds should not collide like this. She doesn't need to know everything I do. I'm in middle school now and she needs to respect that. So now I have to look up all my friends again and start all over building a following. Okay, if Mom doesn't know better than to stalk me online I will remove her portal to do so. Sorry, not sorry, Mom. I might make my new name Wonder Woman because like her I have to have a secret identity to keep people from finding out who I really am. Parents! Sometimes you just have to show them a little tough love for their own good!

(CYNTHIA storms off.)

Scene Thirty-Two

(**ABBY** *and* **CHARLOTTE** *enter. They wear similar clothing and matching eyeglasses.*)

ABBY. She's Charlotte.

CHARLOTTE. And she's Abby.

ABBY. We've been best friends...

CHARLOTTE. ...Forever. And we will be best friends...

ABBY. ...Forever plus!

CHARLOTTE. I wasn't nervous about coming to...

ABBY. ...Middle school...because I knew that Charlotte and I...

CHARLOTTE. ...Would be together and that would make it...

ABBY. ...Easy and...

CHARLOTTE. ...Fun!

ABBY. We have the same...

CHARLOTTE. ...Schedule. We have the same...

ABBY. ...Classes.

CHARLOTTE. And we're in the same...

ABBY. Clubs.

CHARLOTTE. We do everything together and also we're dating...

ABBY. ...Twins. Chad and...

CHARLOTTE. ...Brad Winslow.

ABBY. They're cool but boys are so...

CHARLOTTE. ...Temporary.

ABBY. I'd rather hang out with Charlotte.

CHARLOTTE. And I'd rather hang out with Abby.

ABBY. We've planned a future together. After we graduate high school...

CHARLOTTE. ...We're going to go to the same college.

ABBY. And take the same classes there.

CHARLOTTE. It's like they say, you're lucky if in this life you have...

ABBY. ...One good and true friend.

CHARLOTTE. Like Abby.

ABBY. Like Charlotte.

CHARLOTTE. I am convinced that we have a psychic connection.

ABBY. That's right. Hey Charlotte, where am I thinking we should go right now?

ABBY & CHARLOTTE. Library!

ABBY. She's Charlotte.

CHARLOTTE. And she's Abby.

ABBY. We've been best friends...

CHARLOTTE. ...Forever. And we will be best friends...

ABBY. ...Forever plus!

(They exit together.)

Scene Thirty-Three

(**ANTHONY** *enters to do another video selfie. Holds his phone up in front of his face.*)

ANTHONY. *(To camera.)* Friday, April sixth, 2:15 p.m. For the first time ever I totally nailed my class pictures. Best ever. I look like a regular movie star in them.

(Beat.)

Memo to self, insert "jpeg" of my headshot later.

(Beat.)

I usually have to hide my class pictures, not this year. Everybody I've ever met is getting one!

(**ANTHONY** *exits.*)

Scene Thirty-Four

(CAMRYN and JESSICA are stage left. DEVIN and HENRY enter stage right and stop.)

DEVIN. Hang on it's Camryn.

HENRY. So?

DEVIN. So I heard she broke up with Will and now's my chance to ask her out before someone can beat me to it.

HENRY. Are you nuts?

DEVIN. I think we have some chemistry.

HENRY. Chemistry maybe. But a chance at romance? No way. You've never even been on a date.

(Scene shifts over to CAMRYN and JESSICA.)

JESSICA. Hey Camryn. I think your boy crush is eyeing you.

CAMRYN. Oh my god, Devin is like so cute.

JESSICA. Maybe.

CAMRYN. What do you mean, maybe? Tell me you wouldn't fully go with him.

JESSICA. No way, he's just a boy.

CAMRYN. He's my kind of boy!

(Back to DEVIN and HENRY.)

HENRY. Maybe there's a reason Will dumped her. Girls always have issues, especially thirteen-year-olds.

DEVIN. Why thirteen-year-olds?

HENRY. Because they just became a "teenager" and not sure if they're still little girls or full-fledged women.

DEVIN. I don't know; she seems pretty together to me.

HENRY. Puppy love my friend. That's all that it is. Besides you're only twelve and it's just not socially acceptable to mix grades and ages.

DEVIN. That's stupid. Besides I'm going to be thirteen next month. I just started school later than most or we'd be in the same grade.

(Back to CAMRYN and JESSICA.)

JESSICA. You're older than he is, Camryn. Not good. You're old enough to be his aunt.

CAMRYN. You're being ridiculous.

JESSICA. Oh yeah, what if you want to go to a PG-13 movie. You'll have to pretend you're the adult who is guarding his sensitive eyes and ears.

CAMRYN. I don't think so; he looks a lot older...at least fourteen.

JESSICA. And look who he's hanging out with...that loser Henry Goldner. I hate that guy.

CAMRYN. Why?

JESSICA. He's so immature. Came up behind me last week and pulled my hair. And last year he squirted me with a water pistol.

CAMRYN. He's kinda cute, too...but not as cute as Devin.

JESSICA. Your brain train is completely derailed.

(Back to **DEVIN** *and* **HENRY.***)*

HENRY. And she's best buds with Jessica. Total witch!

DEVIN. Jessica? No, she's nice. She lives two houses down from me.

HENRY. You're delusional.

DEVIN. Stop harshing my hope. I'm going for it...

*(***DEVIN** *walks nervously toward* **CAMRYN** *and* **JESSICA.***)*

JESSICA. He's coming over here. You'd better go girl while you can.

CAMRYN. No way.

*(***DEVIN** *has arrived.)*

DEVIN. Hey Camryn...hey Jessica.

CAMRYN. Hi Devin...uh... I heard you scored a home run yesterday.

JESSICA. *(Cough.)* Jock! *(Cough.)*

DEVIN. Yeah, it was a fast ball and I connected pretty good on it...and...um...I was wondering, do you want to go to the dance next Saturday?

JESSICA. No she doesn't.

CAMRYN. Yes, I do! I mean I'd love to.

DEVIN. Cool. So...okay.

> *(Awkward pause, then he starts to cross back to **HENRY**.)*

CAMRYN. Hey, Devin, I'm gonna go get some juice in the cafeteria. Wanna come with me?

DEVIN. Sure!

> *(They head off together, much to **JESSICA** and **HENRY**'s disbelief. **HENRY** crosses over to **JESSICA**.)*

HENRY. That is so wrong.

JESSICA. Like really.

HENRY. She's just on the rebound from Will and is desperate.

JESSICA. Yup. She's like a relationship junkie. Can't stand being solitary.

HENRY. Good point.

JESSICA. Screws up my plans because the two of us were going to the dance together to scope out guys.

HENRY. Yeah, me and Devin were going to hang out there, too. *(Quickly.)* You know, to score babes.

JESSICA. *(Rolls eyes.)* Babes.

> *(They look at each other for a minute.)*

HENRY. So, uh, you want to go to the dance with...

JESSICA. *(Cutting him off.)* Fine...but no squirt guns and no hair pulling or I'll kick you right in your boy berries.

> *(**JESSICA** heads off. As she exits:)*

HENRY. Great...I'll pick you up at...seven?

JESSICA. Whatever.

> *(**HENRY** smiles, decides not to push his luck, and exits in the opposite direction.)*

Scene Thirty-Five

(**EMMA** *enters.*)

EMMA. There's an old saying my Grandpa Richard uses all the time: "Children should be seen and not heard." He always laughs because he says it as a joke, but that old saying couldn't be truer when it comes to describing my presence at this school. Even though I've had perfect attendance, no one really knows who I am. Imagine that. Fifty minutes an hour, seven hours a day, five days a week, four weeks a month, nine months a year...I was here. Yet I only spoke when I had to, never socialized with anyone, and never joined a club. My grades are perfect and it's not like anyone really disliked me or thought I was weird. I just kept to myself and everyone pretty much let me do that. Mrs. Orson did take an interest in me and she tried to get me to open up, but with all the other students fighting for her attention, she just gave up after a while. Well, I plan on making some major changes next year in high school. Things are going to be a lot different there as I make my move to be somebody. I plan on going to all the dances, running for class president, being in the drama club, playing sports, and every other activity that I have time for. You see, some kids start out reckless and loud and never understand the big picture because they are too busy being in the world to notice the details of that world. Not me, I chose to be an observer. Up until now I've kept my eyes and my ears open to everything and everyone around me. And it's time to use that to my advantage. This flower is about to bloom. Today I proclaim to the universe and my Grandpa Richard that I, Emma, will be seen and will be heard!

(*She exits.*)

Scene Thirty-Six

*(**KATHERINE** enters. She is wearing a graduation cap and gown. She adjusts her cap as we see **ALLEN** enter. He also wears a cap and gown, but they appear to be about five sizes too big.)*

ALLEN. Well at least you got the right size. I think this one was worn by an NFL linebacker or something.

KATHERINE. Good thing we only have to wear them for a few hours.

ALLEN. I might not return it…my dad could use it as a cover for his boat.

KATHERINE. I can't believe we're finally getting out of this place.

ALLEN. I can't believe that they are going to have a graduation ceremony. It's only middle school. We're still just sitting at the kiddie table. The only real graduation is high school graduation.

KATHERINE. Well, that's a long way off for us. And I think they want us to feel like we accomplished something.

ALLEN. Yeah we survived this nightmare…only to jump into an even bigger one. I've heard what upperclassmen do to you in high school. Not pretty.

KATHERINE. It's also for our parents. Maybe this will make them start treating us like adults.

ALLEN. My parents aren't coming. They have weird hours at their jobs…they told me they need to really start earning extra money to pay for my college. Guilt me much?

KATHERINE. Well some kids are having parties and it is one more time when we get showered with cash and gifts from relatives.

ALLEN. Speak for yourself. Although my grandma did send me ten bucks. Whoopee! I'm thinking of investing it in the stock market.

*(Other **STUDENTS** enter the stage, also wearing caps and gowns.)*

KATHERINE. I'm looking forward to high school but I have to say I'm gonna miss this place.

ALLEN. I guess I'm gonna miss it too…a little.

*(**KATHERINE** and **ALLEN** join the other **STUDENTS**, who have lined up across the stage. **ANTHONY**, also dressed in a cap and gown, steps out from the line and crosses down center. His cell phone is now attached to a selfie stick.)*

ANTHONY. This is the last day of school and my last middle school video selfie. I edited together what I had and turned it in to Mrs. Ritter. She gave me a B on it. I shoulda got an A but she said something about it being a little too self-centered. Well, duh! It's about me and my life. I need a good ending for it so I thought for my last one I'd break my format and turn my selfie into a video "ourselvesie"!

*(To the other **STUDENTS**.)* Tighten it up kids, it's picture time!

*(**ANTHONY** punches "record" on his cell phone and holds up the selfie stick. The group of **STUDENTS** bunch up so they are all in the shot. They strike a group pose.)*

Wednesday, June sixth, 7:15 p.m. Ladies and gentlemen, students and parents, I present to you…

ALL. The *[your middle school or junior high name]* class of *[the year]*.

*(He hits the record button. Amid much cheering from the **STUDENTS**, the lights fade out.)*

End of Play

www.ingramcontent.com/pod-product-compliance
Lightning Source LLC
Chambersburg PA
CBHW050303010526
44108CB00040B/2237